Andy Seed

THE ANTI-BOREDOM BOOK OF Brilliant THINGS TO DO

Illustrated by

Scott C

BLOOMSBURY

LONDON OXFORD NEW YORK NEW DELHI SYDNEY

For Alice

Published 2014 by Bloomsbury Publishing Plc
50 Bedford Square, London, WC1B 3DP
www.bloomsbury.com

Bloomsbury is a registered trademark of Bloomsbury Publishing Plc

ISBN 978-1-4088-5076-3

Copyright © 2014 Bloomsbury Publishing Plc
Text © 2014 Andy Seed
Illustrations © 2014 Scott Garrett
Additional illustrations © Shutterstock

A CIP record for this book is available from the British Library.

Printed and bound in Great Britain by CPI Group (UK) Ltd, Croydon CR0 4YY

3 5 7 9 10 8 6 4

IMPORTANT:
Prices and statistics used in this book
are reasonable estimates at the time
of publication.

CONTENTS

INTRODUCTION

This is a book of fun things to do and to talk about. For most of them you don't need anything at all – just a person or two. But if you want to, you can turn to the back of the book where you will find plenty of space to scribble, doodle and write.

This book is perfect if you have a long journey or you find yourself somewhere quiet with nothing to do. It's jam packed with witty jokes, mind-boggling puzzles and challenges, wacky ideas, silly questions, fun quizzes and interesting lists. It is guaranteed to keep you amused for ages!

It is divided into themes with lots of different things to do for each one. There are creative activities, items to choose and score, riddles to solve, games and loads of funny stuff!

So, sharpen up your imagination, prepare to have a laugh, gather your friends or family and get ready to never be bored again!

<<<<<<<<<<<

FOOD

Talk

How do your favourites compare with other people's?
Find out by asking them these fun questions!

What is your favourite...

- Place to eat?
- Pie?
- Fruit?
- Crisp flavour?
- Drink?
- Cheese?
- Biscuit?
- Breakfast cereal?
- Healthy food?
- Cake?

If...

- You could only eat one food for the next year, what would it be and why?
- You never had to eat one thing again in your life, what would it be?

Imagine:

- If you could open a café or restaurant with anyone, who would you choose and why?
- If you lived in the time of Henry VIII and he ordered your head to be chopped off, what would you choose for your last meal?

Fruit and vegetable puns

Have a go at out-punning each other with fruit and veg, for example:

- I'm going to peach you a lesson.
- Don't – I've not bean very well...
- Give me a good raisin not to.
- Lettuce play a different game, go on.

Score

You don't need a pen for these – just read them out and take turns to say your scores:

Rate-a-plate

Give these foods or dishes marks out of ten:

Cabbage

Chilli con carne

Cold pasta

Sticky toffee pudding

Vegetable soup

Custard skin

Boiled eggs and soldiers

Cucumber

Tripe (the lining of a cow's stomach)

Blue cheese

Love, hate or meh?

School dinners

Drinking milk

Supermarket sandwiches

Chopsticks

Pizza Hut

Cooking

Herbs and spices

TV chefs

Reheated leftovers

Indian food

Lists

To read and share. Can you think of any more names?

Tasty people

- Jasper Carrot
- Zoe Salmon
- Sean Bean
- Kevin Bacon
- Alan Sugar
- Titus Bramble
- Meatloaf
- Tim Rice
- Halle Berry

What's in your food?

Substance	Found in	Also used to make
Glycerol	Some breakfast cereals	Explosives
Gum Arabic	Ice cream	Glue
Titanium dioxide	Tartare sauce	Paint
Lactic acid	Yoghurt	Plastics
Beeswax	Liquorice	Furniture polish
Shellac	Jelly beans	Fireworks

Get creative

Launch a sub

Design a new sandwich that's never been eaten before.

If you like, you can draw it here:

Royal nom-nom

If the queen came to dinner and you had to cook, what would be on the menu? It needs:

- Starter
- Main course
- Dessert
- Drink

Crack-a-snack

Think of a new flavour for:

- Ice cream
- Crisps

Jokes

Find out which of these gets the biggest laugh.

Why don't you starve in a desert?
Because of all the sandwiches there.

What's the best thing to put into a pie?
Your teeth.

Why is a tomato round and red?
Because if it was long and green it would be a cucumber.

What do you call a peanut in a spacesuit?
An astronut.

Why do the French like to eat snails?
Because they don't like fast food.

What kind of nuts always seem to have a cold?
Cashews!

What's worse than finding a slug in your apple?
Finding half a slug in your apple.

Challenges

Find out if you can conquer these challenges.

Can you name...
- Ten foods beginning with P?
- Four drinks beginning with L?
- Three sweets beginning with B?
- Four fruits which are yellow?
- Five types of bean?
- Four foods from Italy?
- Three ingredients of shortbread?
- Five ingredients of lasagne?

(Answers on page 145).

Last man speaking: chocolate bars
Take turns to name chocolate bars. The first person who is stuck is out.

Yum scrum
Can you make three foods using the letters of the word PANCAKE?
Answers on page 145.

SPORT

Talk

Time to let everyone have their say. See what happens when you answer these questions as quickly as you can!

Choose....

- Surfing or sailing
- Golf or volleyball
- BMX or rock climbing
- Wrestling or gymnastics
- Horse racing or skiing
- Frisbee or table tennis
- Fishing or rugby
- Karate or rafting

If...

- You could be in the Olympics, what sport would you choose and why?
- You could be a professional footballer, which team would you play for and what position?
- You could go snowboarding with any three people, who would you choose and why?

What's...

- Your best sport to play?
- Your worst sport to play?
- Your best sport to watch?
- Your worst sport to watch?

Score

Find out who rates themselves at different sports and see if you agree!

Dodgy decathlon

Give yourself a score out of ten for how good you are at each event:

Sprint   Javelin   Hurdles   1,500 metres (m)

Long jump   Discus   400 metres (m)

Shot put   Pole vault   High jump

Love, hate or meh?

Archery   Netball   Darts   Cricket

Badminton   Paragliding   Swimming

Ten-pin bowling   Skateboarding   Snooker

Guess

Game, set and whaaaat?

Have fun asking people to guess some facts about the longest ever tennis match and see who's closest. It was between John Isner (USA) and Nicolas Mahut (France) at Wimbledon in 2010. Isner won.

☛ Guess how long the match lasted. (11 hours 5 minutes).

☛ Guess how long the final set lasted. (8 hours 11 minutes).

☛ The first four sets were 6-4, 3-6, 6-7, 7-6. Guess how the fifth set finished. (70-68).

I was a teenager when I started this game.

☛ Guess how many balls were used. (120).

☛ Guess how many pints of water were drunk by the players. (104).

☛ Guess how many aces were served in the match. (216).

☛ Guess how many ball girls and boys were used. (28).

Jokes

Share these hilarious sports jokes!

Q: What's the hardest thing in skydiving?
A: The ground.

Q: Why does the pitch at Wembley have five sides?
A: Someone took a corner.

Q: How does Usain Bolt keep cool?
A: He sits next to his fans.

Q: Did you hear about the athlete who had a fear of hurdles?
A: He got over it.

Q: Did you know I can jump higher than a house?
A: Houses can't jump.

Q: Why did Prince Charles give up polo?
A: His horse had a hole in it.

Q: Why is Cinderella no good at football?
A: Her coach was a pumpkin.

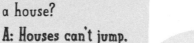

< < < < < < < < <

Challenges

Read these aloud and see if you can work them out together:

Find the intruder

1. One of these is NOT a real sport – which one?

- Noodling
- Snorko
- Wallyball
- Yak polo
- Wushu
- Hooverball

2. One of these is NOT a real sport, either:

- Guts
- Wiffle ball
- Mud bogging
- Bando
- Footjump
- Racquetball

(Answers on page 145).

Last man speaking: ball sports

Take turns to name sports played with a ball. The first person who is stuck is out.

Can you name...

- Four racket sports?
- Three car sports?
- Five horse sports?
- Four board sports?
- Three air sports?

(Answers on page 145).

> > > > > >

Lists

How to say 'football' across the globe

See if people can identify the language:

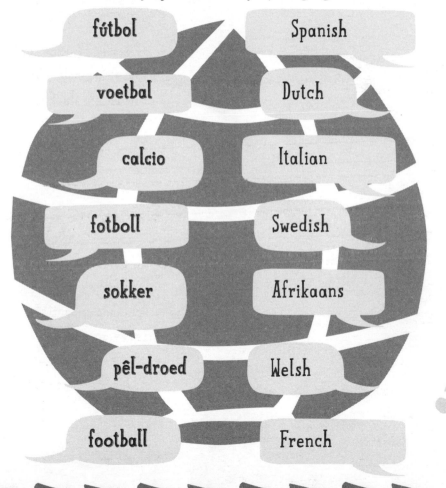

fútbol — Spanish

voetbal — Dutch

calcio — Italian

fotboll — Swedish

sokker — Afrikaans

pêl-droed — Welsh

football — French

Worst excuses for losing

These are all real excuses reportedly made by famous sports stars, but are they good or bad? You decide.

Cricket
My shirt was
too tight.

Football
I was blinded by
the sun reflecting
off a bald head.

Baseball
My eyelid was
stuck open so I
couldn't blink.

Tennis
My opponent
farted when
serving.

Get creative

Say these out loud or write and draw in the back of the book if you like.

Oh-lympics?

Make up some brand new silly Olympic events like these examples:

- 99m sprint
- Gatelifting
- Synchronised murmuring

Nutty nicknames

The top professional darts players have peculiar nicknames, such as:

- Andy 'The Viking' Fordham
- Chris 'Mace the Ace' Mason
- Dennis 'The Menace' Priestley
- Dave 'Chizzy' Chisnall

Think up some suitable darts nicknames for your friends or family.

Kit me quick

Choose a sport then design a spectacular new kit for it.

NAMES

Talk

Stop calling me Shirley

This is guaranteed to produce an interesting discussion...

- If you had to have a new first name, what would you choose?
- What middle name would you have?
- What's the worst name you could have?
- If you changed your surname, what would you go for?

Choose

Talk through these and see if you agree with everyone else:

What would you rather be called?

Boys

- Albert or Gunter?
- Tim or Percival?
- Konrad or Elroy?
- Remington or Jace?
- Dexter or Milo?
- Buddy Bear or Zuma?

Girls

- Ivy or Sybil?
- Betty or Lulu?
- Jayleen or Cordelia?
- McKinley or Dee?
- Angelique or Prudence?
- Apple or Daisy Boo?

Score →→→ →→→→

Nutty names

These are all real names of people from official records in the UK and USA. Give them each a score out of ten for nuttiness:

Festus Flipper

Magic Muxworthy

Peter Piffle

Cicero Booboo

Vanity Quackenbush

Cosmo Crump

Nannie Wham

Dandridge Crumpecker

See who can come up with the best nutty name.

Lists

Sportswear name origins

Quiz your friends and family on these:

Fila®	Named after the Italian Fila family who started the company.
Hi Tec®	An abbreviation for High Technology.
Adidas®	The founder, Adolf Dassler, used a short version of his name: Adi Das.
Reebok®	A reebok is a type of speedy African antelope.
Nike®	Nike was the Ancient Greek goddess of victory.
Puma®	Named after the powerful big cat.
Asics®	Short for *anima sana in corpore sano*, (Latin for 'a healthy mind in a healthy body').
Kappa®	The tenth letter of the Greek Alphabet.
Umbro®	A shortened version of Humphrey Brothers, the people who founded the business.
Le Coq Sportif®	French for 'the athletic cockerel'.
Ellesse®	Based on LS – the initials of the firm's founder, Leonardo Servadio.

Challenges

Are you up to taking on these talking challenges? If you want to write you can use the back of the book.

One name's enough

Some famous people are known by just a single name.

History	Pop	Fictional
Cleopatra	Elvis	Hamlet
Boudica	Sting	Gandalf
Rembrandt	Beyoncé	Tinkerbell
Napoleon	Adele	Electra

Can you think of any more famous men or women known by one name?

Name some names

• Can you think of six girls' names beginning with D?

• Name eight boys' names beginning with E?

• Who can think of the most girls' names beginning with P?

• Who can list the most boys' names beginning with K?

(Answers on page 146).

23

Games

Alphabetical disorder

You can change the rules of these games to suit whoever you are with.

Say it

- Take turns to each say a different name beginning with A.
- Anyone who is stuck loses a life (you have three lives each).
- The next person starts with the letter B, then the next person starts with C, and so on.
- The winner is the one with the most lives left at Z.

Example with two people:

Person one says Adam; person two says Alice; person one says Annette; person two is stuck so loses a life; person two then goes on to B and says Brenda, and so on.

List it

This is a different version that you could play with pen and paper.

- Each person writes the alphabet in a vertical column on the paper.
- For each letter of the alphabet, write a girl's name and a boy's name (don't tell anyone).
- The idea is to think of unusual names.
- Mark the names at the end: you get one point for each name that no one else has got.
- Add up the points to see who wins.

Jokes

See if people can work
these out:

What do you call a man with...

The sun on his head?	Ray
A film award on his head?	Oscar
A beach on his head?	Sandy
A shark on his head?	Finn
Vomit on his head?	Chuck
A treadmill on his head?	Jim
An invoice on his head?	Bill
A block of flats on his head?	An ambulance!

What do you call a woman with...

Nuts on her head?	Hazel
A car on her head?	Minnie
Some monks on her head?	Abbey
Fish on her head?	Annette
A river on her head?	Brooke
A sunlamp on her head?	Tania
Traffic lights on her head?	Amber

MONEY

Talk

These are fun to chat about with friends – or even brothers and sisters...

Loads of dosh

- If you were a billionaire, what would you spend your money on?
- What will you definitely NOT waste your money on when you're older?
- How much pocket money/allowance do you think you should get?

Share it out?

If you were rich, who would you give money to?

→ Your family?

→ Your friends?

→ Homeless people?

→ Charities?

→ A big TV appeal like Children in Need?

→ Everyone?

→ No one?

Score

How do your ratings compare with everybody else's? Only one way to find out: talk these over.

Waste of money?

Give each of these a score out of ten:

Designer labels

Personalised car registrations

Space exploration

Slot machines

Bottled water

Fireworks

Lottery tickets

Fair price?

How much do you think these *should* cost?

A banana   A large pizza   A pet wolf   A big TV

A holiday in Australia   A Diary of a Wimpy Kid book

A jetski

A ticket to a Premier League footy match

Choose

Have fun finding out what everyone would pick:

Spend, spend, spend
But on what?

Sweets	or	drinks?
Books	or	music?
Cinema	or	DVD?
Clothes	or	toys?
Theme park	or	seaside?
Phone	or	camera?
iPad	or	bike?
Presents for friends	or	presents for yourself?

Playthings of the rich

Yacht	or	**speedboat?**
Helicopter	or	private jet?
Mansion	or	**castle?**
Stretch limo	or	Porsche?
Skyscraper	or	**private island?**
Riding stables	or	ice rink?
Swimming pool	or	**personal cinema?**
Butler	or	P.A. (personal assistant)?

Mini-quiz

How good are you with money?

Take this fool-proof test and find out.

1. Where do you keep your money?
a) On the floor. b) In a purse/wallet.
c) In a secret Swiss bank, guarded by henchmen.

2. Granny gives you a £20 note for your birthday – what do you do with it?
a) Make a paper plane.
b) Stick it in your back pocket.
c) Lend it to your brother at 60% interest.

3. How many bank accounts do you have?
a) Eh?
b) I'll get one when I'm 18.
c) I'll call my accountant and find out.

4. How would you use a credit card if you had one?
a) It's party time!
b) I'd buy the occasional hat.
c) As part of a full portfolio of financial options.

5. If you had £500, what would you spend it on?
a) Paying off my debts.   b) Pies.
c) Shares on the Tokyo Stock Exchange.

6. What's your piggy bank made of?
a) Chocolate (well, it was...)
b) Cardboard.
c) Steel and concrete, with a high-voltage laser security system.

What your score means:
Mainly As:
Don't count on becoming Chancellor of the Exchequer.
Mainly Bs:
You're OK with money.
Mainly Cs:
Erm, can I borrow a couple of thousand?

Lists
Funny money

Some of world's currencies with interesting names:

Bhutan: **Ngultrum**

Botswana: **Pula**

Costa Rica: **Colòn**

Guatemala: **Quetzal**

Haiti: **Gourde**

Laos: **Kip**

Malaysia: **Ringgit**

Mongolia: **Tugrik**

Tonga: **Pa'anga**

Tanzania: **Shilling**

Vietnam: **Dong**

Get creative

Make notes

Bank notes like the fiver and tenner have pictures of famous historical people on them. But what if they didn't?

• Design a bank note with you on it: the design should reflect your personality if possible. Choose a note for £5, £10, £20, £50 or a new amount.

• Alternatively, design a bank note with a picture of someone else, for example:

- **A celebrity**
- **A cartoon character**
- **A superhero**
- **A fictional character**
- **A friend or family member**

Chopin Liszt

Make a fun shopping list for a famous person such as a composer, a cartoon character, an infamous criminal, a footballer or a superhero.

Guess
Nearest wins

Ask your friends and family to guess the rough price of these items. The person who is closest to the listed amount below wins.

Beginner's drum kit
Answer: £230

Packet of Jammie Dodgers
Answer: £1.99

Two-hour space flight on Virgin Galactic
Answer: £150,000

Aga cooker (gas, 2-oven)
Answer: £8,000

Pot-bellied piglet
Answer: £50

Star Trek pizza cutter
Answer: £25

Rolls Royce Phantom Coupé
Answer: £334,000

Hot-air balloon flight (one hour)
Answer: £100

Whoopee cushion
Answer: £1

Van Gogh painting
Answer: £200 million

ANIMALS AND PETS

Talk

Get together with your friends or family and see what you all think:

Get-a-pet

• If you could have any two pets what would you choose?

• What would you call them?

No thanks

• What animals do you really dislike and why?

• Would you ever keep a dangerous pet?

The morph the merrier?

• Would you rather be a bird or a fish? Why?

• Would you rather be a horse or a cat? Why?

• Think up some more pairs like these and ask each other.

Choose

Here's your chance to share your favourites:

Pick one or the other

Cat or dog?
Hamster or guinea pig?
Meerkat or kangaroo?
Lion or tiger?
Dolphin or penguin?

Make up some pairs of your own and ask your friends to pick their favourites.

What's your favourite?

⊙ Mammal?

✦ Bird?

⊙ Reptile?

✦ Fish?

⊙ Insect?

✦ Dinosaur?

⊙ Mythological creature?

✦ Baby animal?

⊙ Animal character in a book or film?

Score

Take turns to say what scores you would give:

Love, hate or meh?

Want to work with beasties? Rate these animal jobs out of ten:

Vet   Wildlife film maker   Riding instructor

Zookeeper   Safari guide   Marine biologist

Sheep farmer   Guide dog trainer

Scare score

On a scale of one to ten, how scary are these for you?

Wasp   Snake   Worm   Wolf

Shark   Crocodile

Spider   Leopard   Headlice   Vampire bat

Lists

Funny fish

These are all real fish with ludicrous names:

Wahoo

Football fish

Powder-blue tang

Slime eel

Bigeye trevally

Sockeye salmon

Hairy angler fish

Spotted sweetlips

Bumphead parrotfish

Leafy seadragon

Rubbish pets

Can you add some more?

→ A dead earwig
→ A plank
→ A humpback whale
→ A T. rex
→ A flu germ
→ A broken biscuit

Games

Play these with two or more people.

Animal chains

- The first person says the name of an animal.
- The second person must say an animal beginning with the last letter of the previous animal.
- For example: cow > wallaby > yak > koala.
- Anyone who is stuck is out.

20 questions

- One person thinks of an animal and the other must work it out by asking 20 questions.
- The questions can only be answered yes or no.
- Example: Jo thinks of owl and gets asked, 1) Is it a mammal? **(No)**; 2) Does it have two legs? **(Yes)** and so on.
- Count how many questions there are: 20 is the limit.

Bird puns

Out-pun each other using the names
of birds. For example:
- Rook at me when I'm talking.
- Wren are we going home?
- Aren't you henjoying this?

True or false?

See who gets the most right (answers on
page 146).
1. Eagle owls can turn their heads
360 degrees.
2. There are more voles in the UK
than people.
3. Hedgehogs are allergic to milk.
4. Goats cannot burp.
5. Shark eggs are called mermaid's purses.

Jokes

Have fun sharing these animal jokes.

What do you do if your dog swallows your pencil?
Use a pen.

Why do seagulls live near the sea?
Because if they lived near the bay, they'd be bagels.

What do you get if you cross a crocodile with a flower?
I don't know, but I'm not going to smell it!

What do you give an elephant that's going to be sick?
Plenty of room.

When is it bad luck to see a black cat?
When you're a mouse.

What do you call a fly without wings?
A walk.

Why don't bears wear shoes?
There's no point – they'd still have bear feet.

Why does a giraffe have such a long neck?
Because his feet stink.

Guess

Ask people to guess the weights of these animals. The person who is closest wins. The chart isn't in kilograms (kg) but in 'average 11-year-old children'...

Animal	Weighs the same as this many 11-year-olds
Gorilla	4
Saltwater crocodile	23
Polar bear	13
Kangaroo	2
Moose	16
Hippopotamus	55
Burmese python	1.5
Siberian tiger	5
Grey wolf (female)	1
Red deer stag	6
African elephant	170
Blue whale	4,000

MUSIC

Talk

Find out if your tastes are the same as other people's:

Select a style
- Jazz or Classical?
- Pop or Rock?
- Country or Dance?
- Folk or Rap?
- Soul or Reggae?

Singers and groups
- Who are your two favourite singers?
- What's the most annoying group and why?
- Which band would you like to be part of?
- Which group has the best name?

Songs
- Which song do you really wish you'd written?
- What's the worst song of all time in your view?

Lists

Six babyish song titles

Amazingly, these were all hits:

Skoobly Oobly Doobob	Ten Years After, 1969
Papa Oom Mow Mow	The Rivingtons, 1962
Bibbidi Bobbidi Boo	Perry Como and The Fontane Sisters, 1949
Woo Woo Train	The Valentines, 1955
De Do Do Do De Da Da Da	The Police, 1980
Ling Ting Tong	The Charms, 1955

Score

Take turns to say your scores:

Love, hate or meh?

The Beatles   Psy   Coldplay   Mozart

Michael Jackson   Rihanna   Queen

Justin Bieber   One Direction   Girls Aloud

How good are you at...

Award yourself an A, B, C, D, E or F:

Singing   Reading music   Playing the recorder

Playing keyboards   Drumming   Dancing

Whistling a tune   Playing the guitar

Games

Here are some musical games to play with other people:

Hum fun

1. Take turns humming a tune and guessing what it is.
2. Here are a few songs to try (some easy, some not!):

* Happy Birthday
* Old MacDonald Had a Farm
* The National Anthem (God Save the Queen)
* The Wheels on the Bus
* Silent Night

* Twinkle Twinkle Little Star
* Ten Green Bottles
* Frère Jacques
* Rudolph the Red-nosed Reindeer
* Roar (Katy Perry)
* We Are the Champions (Queen)

Instrumental

☞ Have a go at imitating some musical instruments with your voice – find out who's best.

☞ Some to try: trumpet, drums, violin, bagpipes, church organ, trombone, tuba, double bass, electric guitar, shaker.

☞ If you are really good, create a 'voice band' and make a tune!

Mini-quiz

Could you be a pop star?

Here's your chance to find out if you have what it takes...

1. What happens when you sing?
a) Glass breaks and babies cry.
c) My friends join in.
d) Simon Cowell arrives with a chequebook.

2. What do people say when you take the microphone?
a) AARRGHH!
b) You could be on telly.
c) WOW!

3. How well do you dance?
a) I'm not sure but people say they don't know me on the dancefloor.
b) I've won a few awards.
c) I give lessons to Beyoncé.

4. What happens when you perform in front of an audience?
a) They run and I hide.
b) I get plenty of applause.
c) The tickets are over £300 on eBay.

5. How would you deal with screaming fans?
a) I would scream too.
b) Sign a few autographs, smile and wave.
c) My agent and bodyguards would deal with it.

What your score means:

Mainly As: Erm, sorry but stardom is NOT around the corner. Or within 5,000 miles.
Mainly Bs: You have potential, so who knows...
Mainly Cs: We're getting the stadium and limo ready for you RIGHT NOW.

Get creative
Stars of tomorrow

Dream up and create your own pop group:

Give the band a new look.

What would it be called?

Design their first album cover.

Who would be in it?

Abstract artists

Have a giggle changing one letter of a singer or band, for example:

Pink Floyd

Gary Barlow

U2

Guns 'n' Roses

The Beach Boys

Olly Murs

Sink Floyd

Gory Barlow

U3

Buns 'n' Roses

The Peach Boys

Olly Purs

Songs with pongs

It's a proper hoot replacing one word from famous song titles with the word 'cabbage'. The real titles are on page 146:

1. 'He Aint Cabbage, He's my Brother'
2. 'The Power of Cabbage'
3. 'Cabbage Makes you Beautiful'
4. 'I Will Always Love Cabbage'
5. 'Tie a Yellow Cabbage Round the Old Oak Tree'
6. 'I Want to Hold Your Cabbage'
7. 'The Story of my Cabbage'

Think of some more! Instead of cabbage you could use cheese or haddock or your own idea.

WORDS
Talk

It's fun to chat about these and share your answers with others. See what happens when you ask someone to answer as quickly as they can.

Pick
• What are your three favourite words?
• Which words annoy you?
• What are your favourite words in another language?

Own up
• What's the longest word you know?
• What word have you heard people use and you've no idea what it means?

Word association
This is a fun game to play with a group of people.
• One person says a word and the next person must say a word that has a connection with it.
• Keep taking turns and see where it goes. Answer as quickly as you can.
• For example: cat – dog – bark – tree – leaf – fall – cut – knife – fork – plate.

Lists

Popular and unpopular words

The Sunday Times carried out a survey to ask readers the words they thought were the most beautiful and those that they disliked the most – here are a few of the answers: do you agree?

Favourites	Least favourites
Whisper	Scrawny
Velvet	Gizzard
Crystal	Snot
Murmur	Carbuncle
Caress	Slop
Melody	Prig
Autumn	Bulbous

How to say 'nose' in 12 languages

nez – French   nariz – Spanish   neus – Dutch

hoc – Bulgarian   orr – Hungarian   burun – Turkish

nos – Czech   naso – Italian   nase – German

pua – Swahili   trwyn – Welsh   nef – Icelandic

Games

Here are some word games to enjoy in a group.

Allit Story

- Each person adds a single word to a story, taking turns to do so.
- Every word must begin with the same letter, so start by choosing a letter.
- Continue until you can't go on then try another letter.

Examples:

A: Alice always asked Aunt Agatha about ancient animals... etc.

P: Painfully, Pete piled pencils plus put plastic pots... etc.

Fortunately, unfortunately

- The first person starts a story with a few words, e.g. 'One day Gran went shopping.'
- The next person must then say 'unfortunately...' and carry on the story, e.g. 'Unfortunately, the supermarket had been taken over by giant octopuses.'
- The next person continues the story with 'fortunately', e.g. 'Fortunately, the giant octopuses were very friendly.'
- The next person begins with 'unfortunately' and so on.

Top and tail

Think of words which begin and end with the same letter, working through the alphabet. Examples:

A – area

B – bib

C – comic

You could take turns saying one for each letter or write them down and score a point for each one that no one else has written.

OR

You could do the same for words that contain aa, bb, cc, etc.

Crackit

This is the same as 20 questions on page 38, but this time you can play it for all words, not just animal names.

• One person thinks of a word and the others must work out what it is using questions.

• **The person can only answer 'yes' or 'no'.**

• Only 20 questions are allowed.

Abbreviation creation

Give new meanings to some common abbreviations. For example, does VAT mean Value Added Tax or Voles Are Trouble? Does GPS mean Global Positioning System or Grannies Pedal Slowly? Create some new meanings for these (the real meanings are on page 146):

DIY   VAT

USA   PIN

MP   CIA

ITV   NASA

UFO   RSPCA

Slaying a saying

Here are some well-known sayings, proverbs and expressions. Give them some new endings (a fun example is given for each, with the real word in brackets):

A leopard cannot change its... underpants (spots).

One swallow doesn't make a... decent curry (summer).

Richard of York gave battle in... tights (vain).

The straw that broke the camel's... train set (back).

Children should be seen and not... invisible (heard).

The customer is always... Welsh (right).

Many hands make light... bulb (work).

Never look a gift horse in the... kitchen (mouth).

The early bird catches the... cold (worm).

You can take a horse to water but you can't make it... prime minister (drink).

Challenges

You need a pen for some of these: turn to the back of the book for space to write.

Word grids

Can you make up squares like these? All the words must be different.

2 x 2

I	T
N	O

3 x 3

S	A	P
I	C	E
T	E	N

4 x 4

F	E	A	T
R	A	R	E
O	R	E	S
G	N	A	T

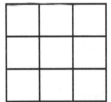
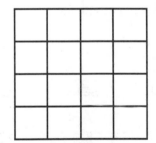

Alphabet race

On a car journey, can you find all 26 letters of the alphabet on road signs or signs on buildings and shops? Who can do it first? You may need to write them down and tick them off. J, Q and Z may be tricky!

Challenges

More ideas to stretch your brain! There are empty pages at the back of the book if you need them.

Pangrams

A pangram is a sentence which uses all 26 letters of the alphabet. The challenge is to write the shortest pangram possible. Here are some examples:

Crazy Frederick bought many very exquisite opal jewels.
(47 letters)

**The quick brown fox jumps over a lazy dog.
(33)**

Pack my box with five dozen liquor jugs.
(32)

**Jackdaws love my big sphinx of quartz.
(31)**

How many letters can you do?

Lipograms
A lipogram involves writing something without using a particular letter. A man called Ernest Wright once wrote a 50,000 word novel without using the letter E!

Can you say or write four sentences on a topic without using E?
Ask someone to choose a topic for you.

54

Guess
Obsolete quiz

Can you guess the correct meaning of these old words which are
no longer used? Answers on page 147.

Word	Meaning A	Meaning B	Meaning C
1. Cumsloosh	A huge noise	A saddle for an ox	A person who flatters someone
2. Yex	To annoy	A tool for making holes in glass	Hiccup
3. Purrock	A small field	A mound of heather	Lumps of dirt in a sheep's wool
4. Lunarian	A madman	A member of a secret singing society	An inhabitant of the Moon
5. Nabble	To argue	A type of dried fish	To gnaw something
6. Croodle	To cuddle together	To argue	A candle maker's glove
7. Pubble	A bent coin	Podgy	To walk the wrong way by mistake
8. Keak	To laugh	A leather apron	Fine dust

Get creative

A pen will come in handy here, and you can write in the pages at the back of the book.

Shiny new words

New words are being added to the English language all the time. Recent ones to make the dictionary are:

- **Selfie** (a picture you take of yourself)
- **Merch** (merchandise)
- **Cake pop** (small cake on a stick)
- **Jorts** (denim shorts)

Have a go at making up your own new word. Here are some different ways to do it:

- Extend an existing word, for example, self > selfie.
- Shorten a long word, for example, merchandise > merch.
- Combine two words, for example, jeans/shorts > jorts.
- Mix parts of words, for example, cake/lollipop > cake pop.
- Change one letter of a word, for example, struggle > striggle (has no meaning).
- Don't forget to give your new word a meaning!

Creature?

Perhaps your new word suggests some kind of creature?

Think one up or draw it here:

TV AND FILMS

Talk

These questions will get everyone talking:

Tell us

• If you could go on any TV show, what would you pick and why?
• What are your two favourite films?
• Which TV programmes really annoy you and why?

Film and TV people

• Who are your two favourite actors?
• Who are your two favourite TV personalities?
• Who are your least favourite celebs?

Pick your...

• Funniest film
• Best animation
• Most scary movie
• Favourite baddie

Choose

If it were up to you...

Would you rather watch:

Doctor Who or *Merlin?*

The X Factor or *The Voice?*

Scooby Doo or *Art Attack?*

Horrible Histories or *Tracy Beaker?*

Top Gear or *Masterchef?*

Action films or musicals?

Creepy films or adventure movies?

Cartoons or old films?

The news or CBeebies?

Score

It's fun to get everyone in a group to call out their score in turn.

Rate-a-film

Give each of these movies a score out of ten:

Shrek   The Hobbit   The Incredibles

Harry Potter and the Half-Blood Prince   Up   E.T.

Despicable Me   Ice Age: Dawn of the Dinosaurs

Love, hate or meh?

You've Been Framed   Dennis the Menace

Newsround   Eggheads   Horrid Henry

Pokémon   Neighbours   Deadly 60

Lists

To read, share and enjoy.

Extra buttons you'd like on the remote control

Bring drinks
Shut my brother up
More chocs
Stop the moaning
Do homework for me
Change day to Saturday
Call servant

(Can you think of any more?)

TV titles

Good idea	Bad idea
Big Brother	Big Mother
Doctor Who	Dentist Who
Come Dine With Me	Come Burp With Me
Top Gear	Bottom Gear
Antiques Road Show	Antiques Toad Show
Eggheads	Peaheads

(Can you think of any more?)

Games

Mangled movies

Make some film titles funnier by changing one letter. Here are some examples:

Star Wart (*Star Wars*)

Jurassic Pork (*Jurassic Park*)

Iron Van (*Iron Man*)

Done with the Wind (*Gone with the Wind*)

Winding Nemo (*Finding Nemo*)

The Lard of the Rings (*The Lord of the Rings*)

Boy Story (*Toy Story*)

Now see what you can do with these:

Jaws

The Sound of Music

Peter Pan

Kung Fu Panda

Cars

Night at the Museum

Shark Tale

How to Train Your Dragon

TV shows can be used too!

Last man speaking

Take turns to name characters from *The Simpsons*. Anyone stuck is out.

Mini-quiz

Just how square are your eyes?

Find out if you are a goggle-box maniac with this fun quiz.

1. How many hours a day do you watch the telly?
a) One.
b) Most of them.
c) All of them.

2. What are you prepared to do to possess the remote control?
a) Not much.
b) Ask nicely.
c) Anything.

3. The TV explodes. What do you do?
a) Go on the trampoline.
b) Cry.
c) Watch one of the nine other TVs in the house.

4. Your Uncle Felix buys you a hamster. What do you call it?
a) Hammy.
b) The name of any *Simpsons* character.
c) Whatever — *Deadly 60* is on!

5. What books do you enjoy reading?
a) *Diary of a Wimpy Kid.*
b) *Radio Times.*
c) What's a book?

What your score means

Mainly As:
Wow! Your parents must be proud of you (or you just lost your glasses).

Mainly Bs:
Not bad, there's hope for you.

Mainly Cs:
Whaaat! Put down this book — you're missing the dog food adverts.

Challenges

Challenge your friends or family!

Do you know?

- Three films beginning with P?
- Four TV gameshows?
- A film for each letter of the alphabet?
- Three female actors whose first name and surname begin with the same letter? (Answers on page 147).

Animal stars

Name an animal then see if you can think of an animal character from film or TV to match, for example:

Mouse – Jerry
Gorilla – King Kong
Elephant – Dumbo
Lion – Aslan

Film Chains

- A challenge for two or more people.
- The first person names a film.
- The next person must name a film beginning with the last letter of the previous film, and so on.
- Example: *Bambi* › *Indiana Jones and the Temple of Doom* › *Monsters vs Aliens* › *Star Wars*, etc.

SCHOOL
Talk

It's good fun to compare answers:

School daze
⊙ What's the best and worst thing about school and why?
⊙ If you could make one change to improve your school, what would it be?

That'll teach yer
⊙ If you were a teacher, what would you be like?
⊙ How would you make lessons fun?

Tell us...
⊙ Your favourite teacher.
⊙ Your best ever school trip.
⊙ Your most embarrassing moment at school.

Finally
If you could rename your school, what would you call it?

Score

Find out what everyone would score these:

Top marks?

Award each subject a grade of A, B, C, D, E or Z for how much you like it:

Science   History   Computing   English

Music   Design and technology   Maths

Art

P.E.   R.E.

Foreign languages   Geography

Cool dinners?

Give marks out of ten for school dinners:

Hot meals   Salads   Puddings

Choice of food   Value for money

Lists

Share these to find out what everyone thinks.

Things schools don't have any more

Can you think of some more?

- Blackboards
- Needlework
- Inkwells
- The cane
- Cold showers

- Domestic science
- Dunce's caps
- Slates
- A clip around the ear
- Free milk

Lay down the law

What should be a suitable reward for:
- Good work in class?
- Doing well at sports?
- Passing tests or exams?

What should be a suitable punishment for:
- Breaking the rules?
- Being noisy in class?
- Forgetting your homework?

Challenges

Write your own school report

Here is your chance to say what *really* needs to be said!
Just fill in the gaps:

SCHOOL REPORT

_____ has worked very _____ this year.

(Your name)

He/she must improve his/her _____ or there

will be _____.

His/her _____ is good and I was very pleased

when he/she _____ in _____.

His/her attitude is _____and hopefully this

will _____.

Finally, he/she must try not to _____ in class.

Jokes

Entertain your friends or family with these!

> **Why did the echo get a detention?**
> For answering back.

> **Boy: I got told off at school for something I didn't do.**
> Mum: What was it?
> **Boy: My homework.**

> **Teacher: Molly, why did you eat your spelling list?**
> Molly: It was a piece of cake...

> **Teacher: Who invented fractions?**
> Kid: Er, Henry the Eighth?

Teacher: why did you go home early?
Kid: I was trying to make up for being late.

Teacher: I'm shocked – you failed every subject except maths.
Kid: That's because I didn't take maths.

Teacher: Why is this period of history called The Dark Ages?
Kid: Because there were lots of knights.

Kid: The teacher told me off because I didn't know where the Alps were.
Dad: Well next time remember where you put things!

Why doesn't the sun go to university?
It has 10,000 degrees already.

Amazing facts

Unusual teachers

These teachers are all fictional (from books, films and TV) and they are most certainly not dull.

Teacher	School	Info
Miss Trunchbull	Crunchem Hall	Muscular headmistress who flings girls with pigtails out of the school, from the Roald Dahl book *Matilda*.
Mr Kupferberg	Springfield Elementary	A French teacher who can't speak French, as featured in *The Simpsons*.
Mr McNab	Grange Hill	In three years of TV episodes he was never seen, despite being the school's headteacher.
Cuthbert Binns	Hogwarts	From the *Harry Potter* series, a professor who teachers the History of Magic. He is also a ghost.
Millicent Fritton	St Trinians	Headmistress who lets the tearaway pupils run wild at this female boarding school.

Get creative

Change school for the better

Here's your chance to create the kind of school that you want!

Imagine you are in charge of the school:

1. If you could have anyone as a new teacher, which three people would you choose? They can be people you know, celebs or even fictional characters.

2. What new subjects would you introduce?

3. What would dinners be like?

4. What new facilities or equipment would you bring in?

5. What would a typical day for a pupil be like:

9 a.m. _____

10 a.m. _____

11 a.m. _____

12 p.m._____

1 p.m._____

2 p.m._____

3 p.m._____

6. Give your school a great new name.

7. Design an awesome new school uniform.

JOBS

Talk

You'll enjoy discussing these with people your own age –
find out what everyone's ambition is:

Dream or nightmare?

* What is your dream job?
* What is the worst job you can imagine doing?
* Would you like to work in the UK or abroad?
* If you were king or queen, what would you do all day?
* What job do you think you might end up with?

What type of work?

Are these things important to you – yes, no or a bit?

* Doing something practical.
* Being creative.
* Having an office.
* Being outdoors.
* Being involved in a business.
* Helping people.
* Being your own boss.
* Working in a team.

Just for me

Make up a new job that's just perfect for you.

72

Choose ← - - - - →

Compare your answers to other people's or just make your own choices:

Career decision

Would you rather be...

A TV presenter or a professional sports player?

A shop owner or a builder?

An artist or a firefighter?

A dancer or a chef?

A vet or a photographer?

A farmer or a scientist?

A plumber or an accountant?

A lawyer or an engineer?

A doctor or a business executive?

Score

Call these out to discover if other people's scores match yours, or just write down your own ratings:

Rate a profession

Give each of these jobs a score out of ten for how much you'd like to do it:

Designer   Actor

Pilot

Nurse

Computer programmer

Dentist

Teacher

Butcher

Taxi driver

Hotel manager

Author   News reporter

Lists
More jobs

Not sure what you want to do when you grow up? Consider one of these:

Disney character: wear a Donald Duck costume all day at a theme park.

Llama farmer: breed and raise South American woolly animals.

Video game tester: try out new games and suggest ways to improve them.

Chimney sweep: stick brushes up fireplaces and clear out all that soot.

Ghost tour guide: tell stories about spooky places in Britain's ancient cities.

Submarine cook: feed a hungry Navy crew by cooking under the ocean!

Lumberjack: work in the wild outdoors, cutting down trees with noisy machines.

Pearl diver: swim deep down in the sea to collect valuable oysters.

Nicknames for jobs

Do you know any more?

Cop	Policeman
Bouncer	Doorman
Sparky	Electrician
Hack	Journalist
Shrink	Psychiatrist
Chippy	Carpenter
Pen pusher	Office worker
Luvvie	Actor
Cabbie	Taxi driver
Brickie	Bricklayer
Squaddie	Soldier

Challenges

Can you rise to the challenge? Get someone to help you!

Do you know?
- Five careers beginning with T?
- Four army officer ranks?
- Being a miner is a dangerous job – can you think of three other dangerous jobs? (Answers on page 147).

On the road
Quite a few jobs involve driving. How many can you name? (Answers on page 147).

Job chains
- A game for two or more people.
- The first person says a job.
- The next person must say a job beginning with the last letter of the previous one, and so on.
- Example: baker > rugby coach > health visitor > restaurant manager, etc.

True or false: careers

Are these statements true or not? Share the quiz to find out who is in the know. Answers on page 148.

1. Tree surgeons perform medical operations on branches such as stitching broken bark.

2. Archaeologists mainly travel the world in cowboy hats, carrying whips and discovering temples of doom.

3. Police officers always carry handcuffs when on duty.

4. Wedding dress designers have to be women.

5. Football managers last on average less than two years at a club.

6. To become a theme park designer you need to study Theme Park Design.

7. Comedians mostly start off by doing lots of shows without being paid.

Guess
See who's closest

Ask your friends to guess these:

How much the British
Prime Minister earns.
Answer: £142,500 a year.

How many people work for
Tesco worldwide?
Answer: about 530,000.

What a jagger used to do?
Answer: sell fish.

How long the training is to qualify
as a vet.
Answer: five to six years.

The name of a person who
makes maps.
Answer: cartographer.

What job you can find out about doing
at www.sis.gov.uk?
Answer: working for the Secret
Intelligence Service (MI6).

The minimum wage in Sierra Leone
(per hour).
Answer: 2p.

What are these jobs more commonly known as?
Lunchtime supervisor (answer: dinner lady).
Washroom operative (answer: cleaner).
Information adviser (answer: librarian).
Wet leisure assistant (answer: lifeguard).
Waste management and disposal technician (answer: bin man).

TECHNOLOGY

Talk

Do your friends and family think the same as you? Ask them!

Best and worst

- What is your favourite piece of technology?
- What is the most annoying piece of technology?
- Which invention do you wish had been your idea?

Imagine...

- Name three things you'd love to own.
- What amazing feature would you add to a mobile phone if you could?

Web stuff

- What's your favourite funny internet video?
- What are your top two websites?
- What do you think is bad about the Internet?

Score

Ask your friends to give their verdicts and see if they match yours.

Love, hate or meh?
Are you pleased that we have these inventions or not really bothered?

Toaster

Electric toothbrush

Torch

Central heating

Radio

TV recorder

Vacuum cleaner

Sat nav

Gauge-a-gadget
Give these gizmos a score out of ten for how much you'd like one:

Volcano lava lamp

Remote control fish

Karaoke machine

3D printer

Sonic screwdriver

Telescope

iMusic Hat (with built-in speakers)

Lists

How to say 'mobile phone' when abroad:

Ponsel
Indonesian

Selfoon
Afrikaans

Telefono cellulare
Italian

Mobitel
Croatian

Mobiltelefon
Danish

Telefon bimbit
Malay

Handy
German

Telemóvel
Portuguese

Cep telefonu
Turkish

Farsíma
Icelandic

ffôn symudol
Welsh

Challenges
Good and bad
Can you think of any more like these?

Good invention
Bow and arrow
Bad invention
Bow and marrow

Good invention
Light bulb
Bad invention
Dark bulb

Good invention
Morse code
Bad invention
Horse code

Good invention
Water wheel
Bad invention
Custard wheel

Good invention
Tape recorder
Bad invention
Ape recorder

Good invention
Ballpoint pen
Bad invention
Ballpoint pin

Good invention
Vacuum cleaner
Bad invention
Vacuum dirtier

Good invention
Rubber band
Bad invention
Rubber hand

Get creative

Abbreviation creation

Technology is full of abbreviations like GB (GigaByte) and PIN (Personal Identification Number) but it's fun to pretend that these stand for something else:

RAM	Really Angry Mice
ISDN	It Still Does Nothing
SLR	Stop Licking Rulers
LCD	Ladybirds Can't Drive
HDMI	Heavy Duty Mother-In-law

Have a go at giving some new meanings to these:

GPS   PDF   HTTP   LED

SMS   USB   SIM   JPEG

If you want to know the real meanings they're on page 148.

Guess

Technology timeline

You could ask people when they think these inventions first appeared and the person who is closest wins.

Telephone	1876	TV	1925
DVD	1995	Pedal bike	1840
Satellite	1957	YouTube	2005
Pocket calculator	1971	Steam engine	1712
World Wide Web	1990	Video game console	1972
Hot air balloon	1783	Aeroplane	1903

Text chex

Here are some figures about text messaging. Ask people to guess the numbers and see who's closest.

Figure to guess	Answer
Percentage of adults in the UK who text each day.	58%
Average number of texts sent per day by 20-year-olds in the USA.	67
Total number of texts sent in the UK per week.	One billion
Average number of words texted each year by 20-year-olds in the UK.	30,000

HOLIDAYS

Talk

Chat, discuss, share, talk, argue, compare, declare and you're there!

Past hols

☞ What's the best place you've ever been?

☞ What's the funniest thing that's happened to you on holiday?

Nightmare hols

☞ Who is the last person you'd like to go on holiday with and why?

☞ What holiday disasters/embarrassments have you had?

Dream hols

☞ Say what your ideal holiday would be in detail.

☞ If you could choose two famous people to go on holiday with, who would they be?

☞ What would your dream hotel have in it?

Score

Giving things a mark out of ten is quite satisfying. You can ask your friends what they think:

Your kinda trip?

Give each holiday destination a score out of ten:

New Zealand   Japan   Bahamas

New York   England   Himalayas   Italy

Antarctic   Paris   Scottish Islands

Order, please!

Put the continents in order of which you'd like to visit the most:

Africa   Antarctica   North America

Australia   Europe   Asia   South America

Choose

This is fun to do in a group, sharing your answers:

Pick-a-place
Choose one from each pair of holidays and say why:

Theme park or safari?

Country or city?

Hotel or castle?

Beach or mountains?

Cruise or activity centre?

Adventure or peace?

Rainforest or desert?

Caravan or tent?

Skiing or white water rafting?

Lists

Can you add some more?
Do you know where they are?
What are your top two?

World famous tourist attractions:

* The Eiffel Tower
* Niagara Falls
* The Great Pyramid
* The Grand Canyon
* Stonehenge
* The Coliseum

UK Theme Parks

* Alton Towers
* Legoland®
* Drayton Manor
* Blackpool Pleasure Beach
* Flamingo Land

Games

Hello, Harry

This game takes some explaining, but it is lots of fun. You will need two or more players, some small round stickers or a pen.

⊙ Everyone sits in a circle; the oldest person says to the person on his/her left, 'Hello, Harry.'

✪ The person who is spoken to must reply, 'Yes, Harry?'

⊙ The first person who spoke then replies, 'Tell Harry.'

✪ The second person then turns to the person on his/her left and says, 'Hello, Harry.'

⊙ That person must reply in the exact same way as before, and the whole cycle keeps repeating.

✪ Have a couple of practise rounds then play for real. Anyone who makes a mistake gets a spot – a sticker on the nose, or a dot with a biro. Now here's the tricky part...

⊙ Anyone with a sticker/dot on the nose is no longer called Harry but 'One Spot'. So, the person talking to him/her must say, 'Hello, One Spot,' etc.

✪ Two mistakes and you're called 'Two Spot'. You only have three lives and you're out: no 'Four Spots!' The winner is the last one in.

Amazing facts

These are fun to share or to get people to guess the figures.

Five long walks
Fancy a stroll?

Route	Length	Approx. time to complete
Land's End to John O'Groats	1,060 miles	54 days
New York to San Francisco	2,930 miles	25 weeks
Cairo to Cape Town	4,500 miles	9 months
Montreal to Rio de Janeiro	5,100 miles	10 months
Rome to Shanghai	5,700 miles	1 year

The heights of famous buildings in popular snack foods

Great Pyramid of Giza	5,346 Snickers bars
Eiffel Tower	32,400 wine gums
St Paul's Cathedral	9,250 Jammie Dodgers
Empire State Building	44,300 onion rings
Sydney Opera House	1,348 packets of Nik Naks
Taj Mahal	2,993 fig rolls

BOOKS

Talk

Asking your friends and family these questions is a great way to find out about some top reads:

Show some character

- If you could be a character in a book, who would you be?
- **Who is your top hero/heroine in a story?**
- Who is your number one baddie and why?

Best books

- What are your favourite three books ever?
- **Who is your number one author?**

Fictional fun

Now have fun continuing this story outline...
- **A mysterious parcel arrives at Granny's house.**
- It's addressed to her new next-door neighbour, Mr Evans.
- **She takes it round, but looking through the window, sees him shouting down the phone.**
- He opens the door and Granny smells chocolate then hears a deep rumble...

Score

Say your scores with friends/family/others, or write them down:

Library grades

How much do you like each of these types of books?
Give them a score out of ten:

Adventure stories   Picture books

Myths and legends

Graphic novels   Science-fiction tales

Mysteries   Animal stories   Diaries

Poetry   Biographies   Puzzle books

Joke books   Information books

History books

TV/film tie-ins   Sport annuals

Lists

Bestsellers

These are some of the most popular children's authors ever –
how many of their books have you read?

Author	Popular title or series
Enid Blyton	*The Famous Five*
Dr Seuss	*The Cat in the Hat*
JK Rowling	*Harry Potter*
RL Stine	*Goosebumps*
CS Lewis	*The Chronicles of Narnia*
Beatrix Potter	*The Tale of Peter Rabbit*
Astrid Lingren	*Pippi Longstocking*
Roald Dahl	*Matilda*
Jacqueline Wilson	*The Story of Tracy Beaker*
Francesca Simon	*Horrid Henry*
Lemony Snicket	*A Series of Unfortunate Events*
AA Milne	*Winnie the Pooh*
Dav Pilkey	*Captain Underpants*

Games

Books that didn't quite make it

Can you add any more to this rather silly list? The real titles are in brackets.

⊙ **The Lion, the Witch and the Bathroom Cabinet**
(The Lion, the Witch and the Wardrobe)
⊙ Charlie and the Cauliflower Factory
(Charlie and the Chocolate Factory)
⊙ **We're Going on a Sock Hunt**
(We're Going on a Bear Hunt)
⊙ The Hitchhiker's Guide to Grimsby
(The Hitchhiker's Guide to the Galaxy)
⊙ **The Well-fed Caterpillar**
(The Hungry Caterpillar)
⊙ How to Train Your Earwig
(How to Train Your Dragon)
⊙ Little House on the Bus Lane
(Little House on the Prairie)

Challenges

Are you up to the task? Give these a go.

Can you name...

☞ **Three books featuring monsters?**

☞ **Four stories about food?**

☞ **Six series of books?**

☞ **Five Roald Dahl books?**

☞ **Two characters who disguised themselves?**

☞ **Four heroes of Greek myths?**

(Answers on page 148).

Mixed up Fairy Tales

Can you identify the two traditional stories that have been blended to make each of these?

1. Goldilocks and the Beast

5. The Pied Piper of Gruff

2. The Goose and the Shoemaker

6. The Ugly Beauty

3. The Three Little Peas

7. Tortoise in Boots

4. Little Red Queen

8. The Gingerbread Prince

(Answers on page 149).

HOBBIES

Talk

Get talking with someone and find out what they're about!

Hobbies to come

- What hobby would you like to do in the future?
- What hobbies might you do when you are old?

Ugh!

- What is your least favourite hobby?

Choose a tutor

If you were going to learn these hobbies, who would you choose to teach you each one? Celebs or fictional characters allowed!

- Astronomy
- Football
- Flower arranging
- Surfing
- Wood carving

Score

Do your friends' scores match yours? Chat and share or write down your scores in the back if you prefer:

Rate-a-hobby
Give each of these pastimes a score out of ten:

Birdwatching

Stamp collecting

Swimming

Photography

Train spotting

Pony riding

Mountain biking

Learning guitar

Martial arts

Drawing

Yes, no or never?
Would you ever try these?

Marathon running

Knitting

Cheerleading

Seashell collecting

Weightlifting

Beekeeping

Rock climbing

Lists

Hobbies to try one day?

These are unusual, difficult or exciting hobbies you might like to try when you're older.

Snowkiting
Using kite power to glide across snow or ice on a board.

Cosplay
Wearing costumes, meeting other players and acting as characters based on films, comics, etc.

Geocaching
Using GPS (sat nav) technology to find containers hidden in various locations.

Ghost hunting
Investigating spooky places such as old castles for evidence of paranormal goings on.

Metal detecting
Using a special piece of equipment to search the ground for coins, jewels and other items.

Fossil hunting
Searching for the preserved remains of ancient creatures in rocks.

*Never try these without a trained instructor or adult.

Lists

Celebs' hobbies

Find out what famous people reportedly do when they're not on TV:

Mike Tyson (boxer)	**Pigeon fancying**
Halle Berry (actor)	**Plays flute**
Rod Stewart (singer)	**Model railway**
Tom Hanks (actor)	**Collects old typewriters**
Kate Moss (model)	**Makes jam**
Michael Owen (footballer)	**Jigsaws**
Roger Daltrey (singer)	**Fish breeding**
Rowan Atkinson (comedian)	**Racing cars**
Taylor Swift (singer)	**Making snow globes**
Tom Cruise (actor)	**Fencing**
Fernando Alonso (racing driver)	**Magic tricks**

Mini-quiz

Are you a video game nut?

Find out using this ever-reliable set of questions.

1) What's the longest you've ever stayed off your XBox®?
a) I don't have one.
b) A week.
c) Go away, I'm on it now.

2) How many video games are in your cupboard?
a) None.
b) About 15.
c) No idea – they're stored in a warehouse now.

3) How much would you pay for the next PlayStation®?
a) 10p.
b) £249.99.
c) I've sold dad's car on eBay, so anything!

4) What do you do with your Wii®?
a) Flush it down the loo.
b) Angry Birds®, Just Dance®, Mario®, Wii Sports®, etc, etc...
c) Everything.

5) What's your preferred game device?
a) A tennis racket.
b) Smartphone.
c) What platform, genre and version are we talking?

What your score means:

Mainly As:
You are not really into video games are you?

Mainly Bs:
At least you'll have time for other hobbies.

Mainly Cs:
Total nuttiness award. How did you find time to read this book?

Choose

What would you and your friends rather do? Answer as quickly as you can.

You decide

Play piano or sing in a choir?
Collect coins or perform magic tricks?
Grow vegetables or bake cakes?
Go swimming or go karting?
Play golf or do archery?
Build models or dance?
Roller skating or ice skating?

If...

⊗ You had to collect something, what would it be?
⊙ You could only do one sport, which one would you pick?
⊗ You could choose to play any musical instrument, what would it be?

Challenges

Have a go at these challenges, with friends or not. Turn to the back of the book for extra space to write.

Silly or true?

Decide if each of these hobbies is made up or real. Answers on page 149:

1. Gongoozling
2. Splubbing
3. Cat fancying
4. Footbag
5. Bashing
6. Moustachoo
7. Conchology
8. Go
9. Eggboarding
10. Extreme fidgeting
11. Urbex
12. Deltiology

Collecting: good and bad

Add some more to this list:

Good thing to collect	Bad thing to collect
Old books	Old ladies
Polished minerals	Sweaty socks
Panini stickers	Black holes
Pressed flowers	Pressed sausages
Antiques	Used tissues

Jokes

My big sister...

Share these jokes for a laugh, but perhaps not with your big sister...

My big sister likes racing cars. I don't know why because she never beats them.

My big sister decided to play the piano. She lost 2-0.

My big sister's a model. She's 8 centimetres (cm) high and made of wood.

My big sister collects coins. She says she'll soon have enough for a handbag.

My big sister tried free running. She said it was too expensive.

My big sister breeds fish. I wish she'd hurry up and breed chips as well.

SHOPS

Talk

Read these aloud with someone
and compare your answers:

Past purchases

- What's the best thing you've ever bought?
- What's the worst thing you've ever bought?

Best and worst

- What type of shop do you like best?
- Which is your favourite shop and why?
- Which is your least favourite shop and why?
- In your view, what's the best place to go shopping?

Rich kid

- If you had £1,000, what three things would you buy?
- What pressies would you get for your friends or family?

What a waste

- Name three things that adults waste money on.
- Say three things that children waste money on.

Choose

Ask your friends or family what they would pick out of the following:

Pick one

Card shop or joke shop?

Sweet shop or tea shop?

Florists or butchers?

Toy shop or pet shop?

Gift shop or bakery?

Fish & chip shop or bookshop?

My kind of store

Which do you prefer?

HMV or Sports Direct?

Carphone Warehouse or Currys?

ASDA or Oxfam?

Toys R Us or Lego® Store?

John Lewis or Paperchase?

Score

It's really interesting to compare your scores with other people's so read these aloud and take turns to say your marks:

Store score
Rate these shops out of ten:

Argos   Marks and Spencer   Lego® Store

Tesco   Toys R Us   Waterstones

IKEA   Currys   B&Q   Boots

Local shops
What's the...

Best local takeaway?

Friendliest place to buy things?

Best name for a shop?

Shop you'd never visit?

Challenges

Have a go at these and ask other people to help you:

Accessories or Waccessories?

Can you add some more to this loopy list?

Good accessory	Bad accessory
Handbag	Chin bag
Pearl earring	Pearl kneering
Hair clips	Nose clips
Bead bracelet	Weed bracelet
Necklace	Bottomlace

True or false?

Who can get the top score in this micro shop-quiz?
Answers on page 149.

1. Over one quarter of all UK shopping is now done online.
2. Debenhams is older than WHSmith.
3. Sainsbury's runs six colleges to teach food skills.
4. Amazon began as an online book seller.
5. 'Pie shop' in Dutch is schoenwinkel.

Amazing facts

Items you can't buy or sell on eBay

All of these are reportedly banned:

A stolen banana
Truncheons
Snakes
Toenail clippings
A hat owned by Adolf Hitler
The title of Duchess
Wild mushrooms

Bat poo
Used undies
Booby traps
Contact lenses
Cigarettes
Tiger fur

Random shop facts

→ Chiddingstone Post Office in Kent has been a shop since 1593.

→ Backwater Reptiles is an online store that sells alligators.

→ Hoxton Street Monster Supplies in London sells items for vampires, werewolves and more!

→ The world's biggest shopping mall is in Dongguan, China. It has 2,350 stores.

Get creative

Imagine this...

Your shop

Imagine running your very own shop one day...

What would you sell? Prices?

What would it be called?

Who would your shop assistants be?

What would it look like inside?

Design the shop front and create a new logo for your store.

Cheeky change

Change one letter in some names of shops and see what you get, e.g.:

The Body Shop → The Boty Shop

B&Q → B&B

Spar → Spam

Topshop → Topchop

Boots → Hoots

Toys R Us → Boys R Us

Guess

Harrods

See who's best at guessing about the world famous London department store, Harrods (answers in brackets).

- What year was Harrods founded? (1834).

- How many people work at the store? (About 5,000).

- What happened to Harrods in 1883? (It burnt down).

- How many departments does the shop have? (330).

- Which animal did Harrods sell to two Australian men in 1969, which went on to star in a famous YouTube video? (A lion called Christian).

- How many restaurants/cafes does Harrods have? (Over 28).

- Which famous person was reportedly banned from Harrods in 2000? (The Duke of Edinburgh).

- How many customers visit Harrods each year? (About 15 million).

- How much does the store's poshest Christmas hamper cost? (£20,000).

HOUSES

Talk

Time to dust off your imagination and have a good time by chatting over these ideas:

Your ideal room

- If you could have anything new in your bedroom, what would it be?
- Design a perfect room with another person as follows:
- Person A chooses one item to go in an empty room – that item is then 'taken'.
- Person B does the same.
- Continue until you are happy with the room!

Cool house

- What would be your perfect kind of house?
- Where would it be located?
- How many rooms?
- If money was no object, what would you have? (Helipad? Private beach? Moat?)
- Who would you like for neighbours?
- Would you live in a haunted house?

When I'm 64

What sort of place would you like to live in when you're older?
Pick your top two:

- The country
- A city
- Australia
- The mountains
- Near my family
- The jungle
- Mars
- The seaside

Choose

The choice is yours... This is fun to do in a group:

Your preferred residence
Say why you prefer each one:

Log cabin or tepee?

Country cottage or Georgian town house?

Castle or penthouse apartment?

Tent or cave?

Beach hut or house boat?

Mansion or ranch?

Tree house or camper van?

Love, hate or meh?

Conservatory

Games room

Balcony

Jacuzzi

Swimming pool

Wet room

Summer house

Stables

Private cinema

Cellar

Tennis court

Amazing facts

Homes around the world

The smallest house in Britain is less than two metres wide.

You can buy a French castle for around £1 million.

The biggest tree house in the world has ten floors and a basketball court.

Some igloos have windows made from clear ice.

Buckingham Palace has 775 rooms including 78 bathrooms.

Many old cottages in Devon have walls made from mud and straw.

Agecroft Hall is a Tudor manor house located in Virginia, USA. It was built in Lancashire, England, but in 1925 it was sold at auction then taken to pieces and shipped to America where it was reassembled.

Travelling tribes in Mongolia live in traditional yurts which are round huts covered in sheep's wool.

Jokes

Have a laugh with these:

How do you keep flies out of the kitchen?
Put a bucket of dung in the living room.

Why did the house go to the doctor?
Because it had a window pane.

What gives you the power and strength to walk through walls?
A door.

What room has no walls?
A mushroom.

Why is climbing the stairs like travelling by plane?
You go up, there's a long flight and a landing at the end.

Why were you so long in the bathroom?
Hey, I was the same size!

Challenges

Take on these challenges and do your best.

DIY Fun

Can you think of some more potty examples to fill this chart?

Item	Good	Bad
Floor covering	Carpet	Yoghurt
Wall building material	Bricks	Tennis balls
Heating fuel	Gas	Homework
Garden feature	Bird table	Cheese toastie
Things to barbecue	Sausages	Buses
How to remove stains	Use detergent	Use a cannon

Alphabet challenge

Can you think of a type of house or dwelling for each letter of the alphabet?
For example:

A – apartment
B – bungalow
C – chalet

Get creative
The house of the future

Design the house of tomorrow. Discuss or draw what you think it will look like. Let your imagination run riot!

Outside
- What does the front of the house look like?
- What are the features?

Inside
- How many rooms are there?
- Do the rooms have any exciting technological features?

Garden
- What's in the garden?
- What are the features?

Address
- What's the address of your future house?

GADGETS, TOYS AND GAMES

Talk

Have a natter with friends or family about these and
see if you discover something interesting:

Good game
• What are your two favourite
games to play?
• What games are you best at?
• What are your worst games
and why?

Future fun
• Describe a toy that you think
should be invented (hover bikes,
invisibility jacket, time machine, etc.)
• Give your toy a brilliant name.

Toy stories
• What are your three favourite toys?
• What was your most loved toy when
you were younger?

Choose

Do your choices match everyone else's? There's only one way to find out:

What's your preference?

Frisbee or puppets?

Felt pens or jigsaw?

Roller blades or keyboard?

Model glider or magic set?

Jenga® or juggling balls?

Water pistol or snooker set?

Boggle® or Bratz® dolls?

Twister® or radio-controlled car?

Type of toy

For each list, put the toys in order of what you like best:

List one: construction sets, board games, action figures.

List two: soft toys, musical toys, sports/outdoor toys.

List three: puzzles, science toys, video games.

List four: vehicles, dressing up, arts and crafts.

Score

Share these through talking, or jot down your own responses:

Traditional toys: love, hate or meh?

These have all been around a long time:

Hoop   Marbles   Spinning top   Doll   Kite

Wooden blocks   Draughts

Ball

Skipping rope   Toy boat

Rate-a-toy or game

Give these toys a score out of ten:

Connect 4®   Cluedo®   PlayDoh®

Scrabble®   Lego®   Top Trumps®

Chemistry set   Swingball®   Paint box

Lists

Toy crazes

Your guide to when famous toys first became popular.

2000 BC	Stone marbles	1982	BMX Bikes
1000 BC	Kites	1983	My Little Pony ®
1759	Roller skates	1985	Transformers
1902	Teddy bear	1991	Game Boy
1903	Wax crayons	1996	Buzz Lightyear
1908	Plasticine ®	1997	Beanie Babies ®
1925	Electric train set	2000	Scooters
1929	Yo-yos	2006	Doctor Who figures
1931	Scrabble ®	2011	Radio controlled mini-helicopter
1936	Monopoly ®		
1949	Lego ®		
1956	Scalectrix ®		
1959	Barbie ®		
1966	Action Man ®		
1971	Space Hoppers		
1977	Slime		
1978	Star Wars toys		
1980	Rubik's Cube ®		

Games

A classic game to play in a group.

Washing the elephant

⊙ This works best with a big group. You all sit in a circle.

⊙ Four volunteers are chosen to go out of the room.

⊙ The person in charge in the room explains the game: someone must perform a mime, which means acting out a job or action – it must not be very short, and must be carefully mimed.

⊙ When the mime performer is chosen, the first volunteer is called back into the room. She watches the mime in silence. She must then copy the mime for the next volunteer. It's important that the watchers don't say anything.

⊙ This repeats in a chain until all four volunteers have performed the mime – at the end they take turns to say what they thought the action was.

Challenges

Can you take on these challenges and triumph?

True or false?

Answers on page 150.

1. In the 1960s a giant bouncy 'superball' was made for a publicity stunt. It was dropped from a tower block but destroyed a car on its second bounce.

2. A 'joy buzzer' is a joke shop prank device which gives an electric shock to people who shake hands with the user.

3. The teddy bear is named after a U.S. president.

Name that toy

You'll find some answers on page 150.

• Name four toys beginning with T.
• Name three games beginning with B.
• Name five toys which have strings.

Toy chains

A game to play with two or more people:

• The first person says the name of a toy.
• The second person must say a toy beginning with the last letter of the previous toy.
• For example: Barbie ® > Etch-a-Sketch ® > hoop > pogo stick.
  • No repeats allowed; anyone who is stuck is out.

Get creative

Joke shop gems

Look at this list of joke shop items then think up or draw your own prank invention in the box below.

- Stink bomb
- Whoopee cushion
- Itching powder
- Chattering teeth
- Disappearing ink

- Plastic doggy-doo
- Fake vomit
- Fake nail through the finger
- Rubber snake

- Dracula teeth
- Fake blood
- Squirting flower
- Soot soap
- Sneezing powder

Get creative

Better bike

Draw or think up some cool features to make a bike better.

Speed boosters

Fun gadgets

Style elements

Comfort features

Technological improvements

THE FUTURE

Talk

Talking these over with people you know will be really interesting:

Your future

* Where do you want to live when you are an adult?
* What do you hope will change about the world in the future?
* If you had to live on another planet, which one would you choose?

Got no energy?

* If oil and gas run out in your lifetime and you have to use less energy, what gadget would you do without?
* What gadget would you keep whatever?

The aliens are coming...

* If a UFO landed in your garden and the aliens wanted to know about our planet, what would you tell them?
* Where would you take them to show a typical day on Earth?

Choose

It's time to pick your favourite from each pair – it's good to do this with someone you know:

Inventions of tomorrow

⊙ **Hover boots** or **personal robots?**

⊙ **Cheap space flights** or **underwater cities?**

⊙ **Perpetual sun cream** or **x-ray specs?**

⊙ **Wrist TV** or **jet pack?**

⊙ **Time machine** or **invisibility suit?**

⊙ **Everlasting chewing gum** or **auto-restocking fridge?**

⊙ **Gourmet TV dinners** or **healthy cake?**

⊙ **Self-following suitcase** or **digital room tidier?**

Now think of two new inventions that you'd like to have.

Score

Share your scores in a group or keep them to yourself: it's up to you...

What will you look like in the future?

Score these out of ten:

Dyed hair   Smart suit   High heels   Fake tan

Tattoos   Beard/moustache   Cowboy hat

Piercings   Wig   Indoor sunglasses

Select your vehicle

You'll probably want to drive in the future, but what? Pick your top two:

Electric micro-car   Vintage Ferrari

Bus   Humongous 4x4 truck

Old banger   Sleek Mercedes   Convertible sports car

Get creative

Mind your own business

A lot of people start up their own business when they leave school or college. Imagine you have your own company and you are the boss. Discuss or draw:

What kind of business will it be? Will you be making something? Will it be a café? Will you be providing a service?

Imagine or design a logo for it.

Think of a cool name for it.

Future me

Discuss or draw some of these:

A gadget you will own one day.

A piece of clothing that
you might wear in
the future.

What you
will look like
aged 30.

The pet you
might have.

Guess

What does tomorrow hold? Have fun talking over these, or write your ideas down.

What will I be doing?

★ In 5 years' time? ★

★ In 10 years' time? ★

★ In 20 years' time? ★

★ In 50 years' time? ★

Tough decisions...

You'll have to make lots of choices in the future, so practise by deciding which of these you would prefer and why:

☞ To have no loo paper or no toothpaste.

☞ To live with no TV or no computer.

☞ To be stuck in a lift with Homer Simpson or Mr Burns.

☞ That there were no birds or no fish.

☞ That it was never summer or never winter.

MISCELLANEOUS FUN
Talk

Ask someone these then tell them your answers:

I'm the boss
* If you were ruler of the world, what's the first thing you would do?
* What else would you change?
* Would you ban anything?

Super me
* What is your preferred super power and why?
* If you could have two famous friends, who would they be?

Not so super me
* What are your worst habits?
* What's the naughtiest thing you have ever done?
* What's the worst accident you've ever had?

Shipwrecked!
* If you were marooned on a desert island, which three people would you want with you and why?
* What three things would you save from the ship?
* What luxury item would you choose to have on the island?

Diddy you
* What's your earliest memory?
* What kind of baby were you?
* What was your first word? What do you wish it was?

Score

Compare your answers with friends or family:

Best and worst

What's your best and worst....

Colour   Hairstyle   Car   Shoes   Pizza   App

Pudding   Item of clothing   Expression   Pet

Love, hate or meh?

Tattoos   Rap   Motorbikes   Snakes   Christmas dinner

Gardening   Trains   Marmite   Simon Cowell

Be honest

How do you score out of ten on:

Messiness   Loudness   Helpfulness   Stylishness   Silliness

Choose

Do your friends agree with you?
What about your family or other people?

Decide

Cheese	or	fruit?
Scruffy	or	smart?
Be in a band	or	be a sports star?
Cake	or	pie?
Spain	or	Italy?
Mars Bar®	or	Kit Kat®?
Fame	or	fortune?
Vanilla	or	chocolate?
Volleyball	or	chess?
United	or	City?
Lake District	or	Cornwall?
Pins and needles	or	cramp?
Abba	or	The Beatles?
Heatwave	or	snow?
Zoo	or	theme park?
Mercedes	or	Jaguar?
Mars	or	Jupiter?

Games

Here are some great games
for two or more people.

Captions

⊙ **Each person needs a pen/pencil
and a piece of A4 paper.**

⊙ Each person draws a scene in
the top part of the page (take up no
more than a quarter of it). It can be
anything but should feature lots of
detail. It can have people, things,
places, animals or anything in but no
words or letters.

⊙ **Pass the drawings to the left,
do not say anything. Each person
now writes a description of what the
drawing shows, underneath
the picture.**

⊙ Fold the drawing back so that
only the writing is now showing. Pass
it to the left.

⊙ **The next person now draws what
the description says, underneath,
in detail.**

⊙ Fold back the writing so that only
the new picture is showing. Pass it on
and continue until the paper is filled
(it should have four pictures and four
captions).

⊙ **Open out and enjoy!**

Last man speaking

Take turns to name examples of these things. The first person who is stuck is out.

* Vegetables
* Football clubs
* Countries in Europe

Alphabeti-call

Take turns to name one of these beginning with A, then B, then C, and so on:

* Famous people (surnames)
* Famous people (first names)
* Towns or cities

Jokes

A selection of random jokes to share:

How many rotten eggs does it take to make a stink bomb?
A phew.

Did you hear about the twit who keeps going around saying 'no'?
No.
Oh, so it's you!

Did you hear about the little boy that they named after his father?
They called him Dad.

What has a bottom at the top?
Your legs.

What is the best hand to write with?
Neither – it's best to write with a pen.

Why did Jack go out with a prune?
Because he couldn't find a date.

Why was the Egyptian girl confused?
Because her daddy was a mummy.

Will this path take me to the main road?
No, you'll have to go by yourself.

Why does a flamingo lift up one leg?
Because if it lifted up both legs it would fall over.

Mini-quiz

How fit are you?

Write down your answers then find out what your score means:

1. A pizza lorry crashes into your garden, shedding its load. Do you:
a) Chomp your patio clean?
b) Lift a few boxes out of the way and then rest?
c) Carry everything to safety and then repair the fence?

2. Your mum buys a new treadmill. Do you:
a) Laugh a lot then celebrate with caramels?
b) Have a two-minute blast on it while no one's looking?
c) Set the thing to max speed and break a few records?

3. Your teacher asks you to take part in Sports Day at school. Do you:
a) Try and change your teacher's mind?
b) Say you don't mind taking part?
c) Punch the air in triumph?

4. Your friend next door invites you to a party. Do you:
a) Insist that your dad drives you there?
b) Dance for ten minutes then check out the nachos?
c) Turn down the invitation and swim the channel instead?

5. A Frisbee lands at your feet. Do you:
a) Eat it?
b) Wander around for a while trying to find the owner?
c) Show off for an afternoon by catching your own long-distance throws.

What your score means:

Mainly As:
You must be glued to the couch.

Mainly Bs:
At least you walk to the fridge.

Mainly Cs:
Olympic gold is just around the corner...

139

Amazing facts

20 Amusing plants

Shockingly, these are all real names:

Bear's breeches

Bog myrtle

Bunny ears

Cruel plant

Funkia

Giant puffball

Giant spaniard

Living rock

Love-lies-
bleeding

Mind-your-own-business

Nit grass

Old man's beard

Sausage tree

Shaggy ink cap

Stinkhorn

Tumbling ted

Voodoo lily

Wonga-wonga vine

Woolly willow

Challenges

Have a go at these fun body challenges.

Hands up

Stand next to a wall with your arms by your sides. Push the hand which is touching the wall against the wall. Count to 62 while you do this. Finally, move away from the wall and watch your arm mysteriously rise....

Holy hand

Roll up a piece of A4 paper to make a tube. Hold the tube up to one eye and look through it like a telescope. Put your other hand next to the end of the tube, keeping both eyes open. Eek! – is that a hole in your hand?

The floating sausage

Point your two index fingers together on the end of your nose. Look at the fingers and gradually move them away from your nose. When they are a few centimetres away from your nose, slowly move the two fingers apart.
See the sausage?

Challenges
Skillz

How many of these can you do?

1. Cross your eyes

2. Lick your nose

3. Touch your toes

4. Click your fingers

5. Roll your tongue

6. Waggle your ears

7. Pat your head and rub your tummy at the same time

8. Lick your elbow

9. Whistle

10. Juggle

11. Sing in tune

12. Wink

Guess

Annoying riddles

See if anyone can work out these:

What gets whiter the dirtier that it gets?
A blackboard.

What can go up and come down without moving?
The temperature.

What has to be broken before it can be used?
An egg.

How much earth is in a hole six meters deep and two meters wide?
There is no earth in a hole.

What's the greatest worldwide use of cowhide?
To cover cows.

What object has keys that open no locks, space but no room, and you can enter but not go in?
A computer keyboard.

If you have it, you want to share it. If you share it, you don't have it. What is it?
A secret.

Before Mount Everest was discovered, what was the highest mountain on Earth?

Mount Everest.

Can a man legally marry his widow's sister in Ireland?

No, he's dead.

How many times can you subtract the number 5 from 35?

Once, because after you subtract 5 it's not 35 anymore.

What stays where it is when it goes off?

An alarm clock.

How many months have 28 days?

All of them.

What do you throw out when you want to use it, but take in when you don't want to use it?

A fishing line.

A man fell off a seven-metre ladder and landed on the pavement, but he did not get hurt. Why not?

He fell off the bottom rung.

Why didn't Beethoven finish the Unfinished Symphony?

Because it was written by Schubert.

ANSWERS

Food

Can you name...

(page 11) possible answers:

- **Ten foods beginning with P:** potato, peas, pineapple, peach, pie, pickle, pear, pasta, pizza, peanuts, poppadom, pancake, pastry, pepper, pepperoni, pitta, pizza, plum, pork, popcorn, pretzel.
- **Four drinks beginning with L:** lemonade, limeade, Lucozade, lilt, latte, lager, liqueur.
- **Three sweets beginning with B:** bonbons, barley sugar, blackjack, bubblegum, butterscotch.
- **Four fruits which are yellow:** lemon, banana, grapefruit (plus any of these which are sometimes yellow: apple, pear, apricot, peach, plum, melon, mango).
- **Five types of bean:** black, butter, lima, flageolet, broad, kidney, lentil, peas, mung, pinto, soya, haricot (baked beans).
- **Four foods from Italy:** pizza, pasta (e.g. cannelloni, spaghetti, ravioli, lasagne, tagliatelle, tortellini), salami, bruschetta, olives, ciabatta (bread), risotto, ragù, parmesan, mozzarella, ice cream.
- **Three ingredients of shortbread:** flour, butter, sugar.
- **Five ingredients of lasagne:** mince, oil, pasta, onion, tomatoes, carrot, garlic, stock, cheese, milk, butter, flour, herbs.

Yum scrum (page 11)

possible answers:
cake, pea, pecan, cep (a type of mushroom), canapé.

Sport

Find the intruder (page 16)

1. Snorko; 2. Footjump

Can you name... (page 16)

possible answers:

- **Four racket sports:** badminton, squash, tennis, table tennis, beach tennis, lacrosse.
- **Three car sports:** autograss, F1, drag racing, hill climbing, rallying, touring car racing, demolition derby.
- **Five horse sports:** polo, dressage, eventing, gymkhana, horse racing, rodeo, showjumping, steeplechase.
- **Four board sports:** skateboard, surfing, scooter, wakeboard, street luge, snowboard, bodyboard.
- **Three air sports:** gliding, skydiving, base jumping, air racing, ballooning, hang gliding, paragliding.

Names
Name some names
(page 23) possible answers:
• **Girls' names beginning with D:** Daisy, Danielle, Davina, Dawn, Debbie, Denise, Diana, Diane, Donna, Doris, Dorothy.
• **Boys' names beginning with E:** Ed/Edward, Egbert, Eli, Eliot, Ellis, Elvis, Emmett, Eric, Ernie/Ernest, Errol, Eugene, Evan, Ezra.
• **Girls' names beginning with P:** Pandora, Pearl, Penelope, Persephone, Pollyanna, Priscilla, Prudence.
• **Boys' names beginning with K:** Karel, Kaspar, Kay, Keefe, Kelvin, Kendall, Kerr, Kit, Kurt.

Animals and pets
True or false? (page 39):
1. False
2. True
3. True
4. False
5. True

Music
Songs with pongs
(page 47):
1. 'He Ain't Heavy, He's My Brother' by The Hollies
2. 'The Power of Love' by Frankie Goes to Hollywood
3. 'What Makes You Beautiful' by One Direction
4. 'I Will Always Love You' by Whitney Houston
5. 'Tie a Yellow Ribbon Round the Old Oak Tree' by Tony Orlando and Dawn
6. 'I Want to Hold Your Hand' by The Beatles
7. 'The Story of My Life' by One Direction

Words
Abbreviation creation
(page 51) real meanings:
DIY	Do It Yourself
USA	United States of America
MP	Member of Parliament
ITV	Independent Television
UFO	Unidentified Flying Object
VAT	Value Added Tax
PIN	Personal Identification Number
CIA	Central Intelligence Agency
NASA	North American Space Agency
RSPCA	Royal Society for the Prevention of Cruelty to Animals

Obsolete quiz (page 55):
1.C, 2.C, 3.A, 4.C, 5.C, 6.A, 7.B, 8.A

TV and Films
Do you know? (page 63)
possible answers:
- **Three films beginning with P:** *Pinocchio, Pokémon series, Planes, Pink Panther, Popeye, Peter Pan, Planet of the Apes.*
- **Four TV gameshows:** *Eggheads, Countdown, QI, Who Wants to be a Millionaire, The Weakest Link.*
- **A film for each letter of the alphabet** (some answers for the trickiest letters):
- **J:** *Jumanji, Jonny English, Jaws, The Jungle Book.*
- **K:** *The Karate Kid, Kidnapped, Kung Fu Panda, The King and I, King Kong.*
- **Q:** *The Quiet Man, Quantum of Solace.*
- **X:** *The X-Men* series.
- **Z:** *Zulu, Zorba the Greek, Zoolander.*
- **Three female actors whose first name and surname begin with the same letter?** Helen Hunt, Holly Hunter, Keira Knightly, Lindsay Lohan, Marilyn Monroe, Greta Garbo.

Jobs
Do you know? (page 77)
possible answers:
- **Five careers beginning with T:** tailor, theatre manager, textile designer, therapist, tiler, tour guide, toolmaker, tourist information officer, train driver, translator, travel agent, tree surgeon, typist, tyre fitter.
- **Four army officer ranks:** lieutenant, captain, major, colonel, brigadier, general.
- **Dangerous jobs:** coastguard search and rescue, builder, zoo keeper, oil worker, firefighter, window cleaner, power line repair, roofer, police officer, stuntman, fisherman, logger.

On the road (page 77)
possible answers:
- **Jobs involving driving:** taxi driver, lorry driver, tanker driver, bus driver, coach driver, policeman, fireman, driving instructor, estate agent, army truck driver, ambulance driver.

True or false: careers
(page 78)
1. False
2. False
3. True
4. False
5. True
6. False
7. True

Technology

Abbreviation creation
(page 84) real meanings:

RAM	Random Access Memory
ISDN	Integrated Services Digital Network
SLR	Single Lens Reflex
LCD	Liquid Crystal Display
HDMI	High-Definition Multimedia Interface
GPS	Global Positioning System
USB	Universal Serial Bus
HTTP	Hypertext Transfer Protocol
SIM	Subscriber Identity Module
LED	Light Emitting Diode
SMS	Short Message Service
JPEG	Joint Photographic Experts Group
PDF	Portable Document Format

Books

Can you name... (page 96)
possible answers:

• **Three books featuring monsters:** *The Gruffalo, Beauty and the Beast, The Iron Man, Beowulf, Not Now Bernard, Where the Wild Things Are.*

• **Four stories about food:** *Charlie and the Chocolate Factory, The Very Hungry Caterpillar, Six Dinner Sid, Green Eggs and Ham, Ratburger.*

• **Six series of books:** *Narnia Chronicles, Diary of a Wimpy Kid, Goosebumps, Happy Families, A Series of Unfortunate Events, Beast Quest, Harry Potter, Animal Ark, Peter Rabbit, Mr Men.*

• **Five Roald Dahl books:** *James and the Giant Peach, Matilda, The Witches, George's Marvellous Medicine, Esio Trot, Danny the Champion of the World, Revolting Rhymes.*

• **Two characters who disguised themselves:** Count Olaf, Mrs Doubtfire, Odysseus, Spiderman (and many other superheroes), the Prince and the Pauper.

• **Four heroes of Greek myths:** Perseus, Jason, Theseus, Achilles, Orpheus, Hercules.

Mixed up Fairy Tales
(page 97):

1. *Goldilocks and the Three Bears*/**Beauty and the Beast.**
2. **The Goose that Laid the Golden Egg**/*The Elves and the Shoemaker.*
3. *The Three Little Pigs*/**The Princess and the Pea.**
4. *Little Red Riding Hood*/**The Snow Queen.**
5. **The Pied Piper of Hamelin**/*Three Billy Goats Gruff.*
6. *The Ugly Duckling*/**Sleeping Beauty.**
7. **The Tortoise and the Hare**/*Puss in Boots.*
8. *The Gingerbread Man*/**The Frog Prince.**

Hobbies
Silly or true? (page 104):

1. **Real:** gongoozlers are canal enthusiasts.
2. **Not real.**
3. **Real:** cat fanciers take their cats to shows.
4. **Real:** footbag is a 'keepy-uppy' game.
5. **Real:** bashers are rail travel fans.
6. **Not real.**
7. **Real:** conchology is the study of shells.
8. **Real:** Go is an old Chinese board game.
9. **Not real.**
10. **Not real.**
11. **Real:** urbex is short for urban exploration (investigating abandoned buildings).
12. **Real:** deltiology is collecting postcards.

Shops
True or false? (page 109):

1. **False:** it's not as high as that.
2. **True:** Debenhams began in 1778 and WHSmith in 1792.
3. **False:** it runs seven colleges.
4. **True:** Amazon sold only books at first.
5. **False:** schoenwinkel means 'shoe shop' in Dutch.

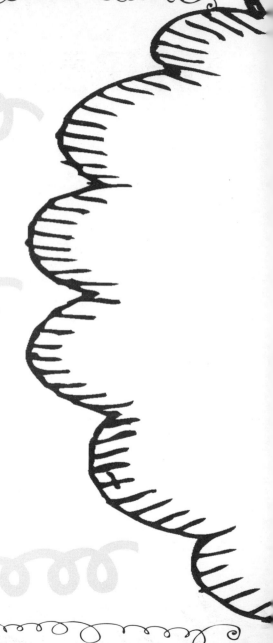

Toys and Games

Name that toy (page 124)

possible answers:

- **Four toys beginning with T:** Transformer, teddy, tea set, Thomas the Tank Engine, train set.
- **Three games beginning with B:** Boggle®, battleships, backgammon, Balderdash®, Buckaroo®, bowls, badminton.
- **Five toys which have strings:** Yo-yo, pull-along animal, marionette (puppet), swingball®, cup and ball, clackers, diabolo, kite.

True or false? (page 124):

1. **True.**
2. **False:** it just vibrates.
3. **True:** the president was Theodore Roosevelt (nicknamed Teddy).

SCRIBBLE SPACE

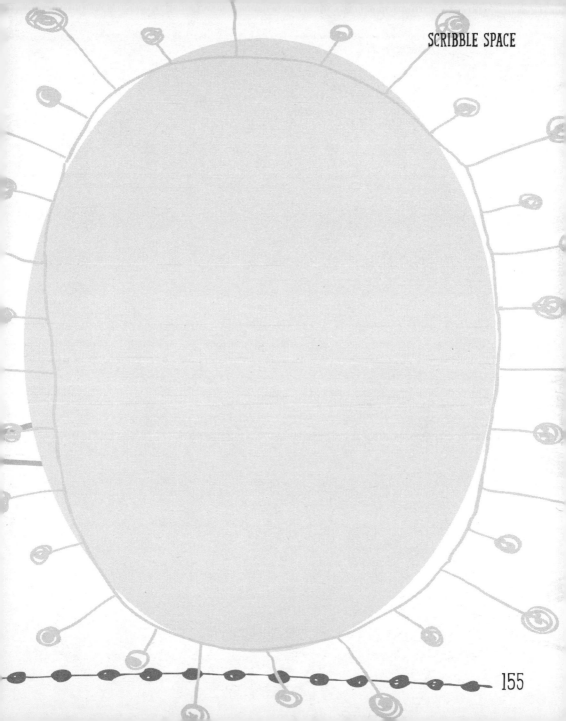

SCRIBBLE SPACE

FURTHER INFORMATION

Books to read

These books have more games, activities and fun things to do:

Magic Tricks to Make and Do by Ben Denne and Andi Good (Usborne, 2011)
The Bumper Book of Very Silly Jokes by Steph Woolley (Macmillan, 2013)
100 Games to Play on Holiday by Rebecca Gilpin and Antonia Miller (Usborne, 2010)

Websites

More cool things to do online:

www.bbc.co.uk/cbbc/games - Loads of fun free games to play.
buildyourwildself.com/ - Turn yourself into a wacky animal!
www.bbc.co.uk/newsround/animals - Amazing true stories, news and videos about animals.

Also Available by
ANDY SEED!
Warning: Contains amazing facts that will make your sides split!

This laugh-out-loud book is bursting with silly lists, facts, jokes and funny true stories all about animals, inventions, food and much more. Find out about The Great Stink, the man who ate a bike, the world's richest cat and a sofa that can do 101mph.

Discover gross foods, epic sports fails, wacky words and even silly things to do... Unmissable!

£5.99

978-1-4088-5079-4